Alex the Food Expert

by Rob Kemp
Illustrated by Julia Castaño

Contents

OXFORD
UNIVERSITY PRESS

Our food and drink are our fuel! They give our bodies energy.

Alex

Alex is a dietician. He knows a lot about the food we eat and how it affects us.

What is a dietician?

Dieticians are scientists. Their job is very important. They tell people how to eat a good, varied and healthy **diet**.

Alex helps people find the right types of food to make them feel better when they are ill. He works with doctors and nurses. He works in schools and workplaces. He also works with families.

Food groups

Alex knows about the different types of food people should eat to stay fit and healthy. He also knows how much of each type of food people should eat every day.

Food is grouped into the following categories:

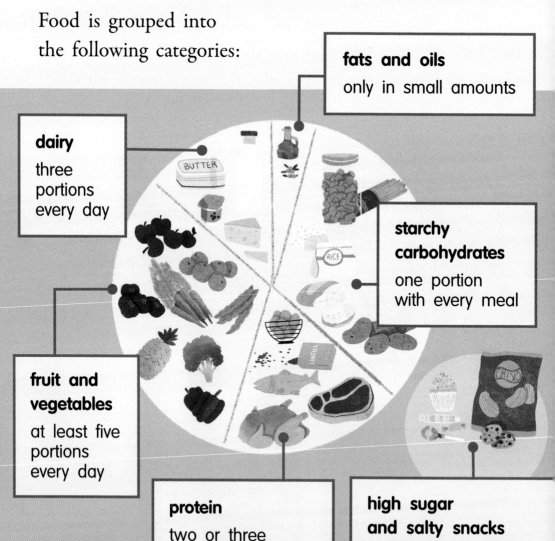

fats and oils
only in small amounts

dairy
three portions every day

starchy carbohydrates
one portion with every meal

fruit and vegetables
at least five portions every day

protein
two or three portions every day

high sugar and salty snacks
only in small amounts

Dieticians like Alex know all about the health benefits of the different food groups.

Food group	Benefit
Starchy carbohydrates	Gives our bodies energy.
Dairy	Keeps our teeth and bones strong and healthy.
Protein	Builds muscles and helps the body to grow and repair itself.
Fruit and vegetables	Keeps our bodies and digestive systems healthy.
Fats and oils	Gives our bodies energy.

Vitamins and nutrients

The food we eat contains a huge variety of vitamins, nutrients and other useful things. Alex tells people how these things help us in different ways and which foods contain them.

Vitamin A:

- found in eggs, butter and oily fish
- good for eyesight and keeping the skin healthy.

Vitamin C:

- found in oranges, strawberries and blackcurrants
- good for fighting off bugs that give us colds and flu.

Fibre:

- found in cereals, fruits and vegetables
- good for your heart and your **digestion**.

Calcium:

- found in milk, cheese and green leafy vegetables
- good for growing strong bones and healthy teeth.

Iron:

- found in red meat, beans, chickpeas and nuts
- good for healthy blood and energy.

Did you know?

They may not be your favourite foods but green and orange vegetables, like broccoli and carrots, are full of vitamins. They help give you energy.

Protein pick-up

Protein helps to keep our muscles strong and gives us energy. Fish, chicken and other lean meats are great sources of protein.

However, many people choose not to eat meat or want to cut down on the amount of meat they eat. Alex explains that you can still get protein from other foods.

How much?

It can be difficult to know how much of each type of food to eat, but Alex can help! He shows people what a 'portion' of lots of different foods looks like.

All these dishes contain one portion for a child aged 10.

3 tablespoons of cooked pasta

2 small potatoes

90 grams (g) of cooked chicken

1 slice of bread

2–3 fish fingers

200 millilitres (ml) of milk

1 medium apple

7 cherry tomatoes

Five a day

Alex knows that it is important to eat at least five portions of different fruits and vegetables a day. He also knows that not everyone likes eating vegetables. He tells people about different ways to cook healthy foods to make them more appealing.

Have you ever tried roasting carrots with a little honey? They are delicious!

Why is water best?

We need to drink plenty of fluids. Alex tells people to drink around six to eight glasses of water each day.

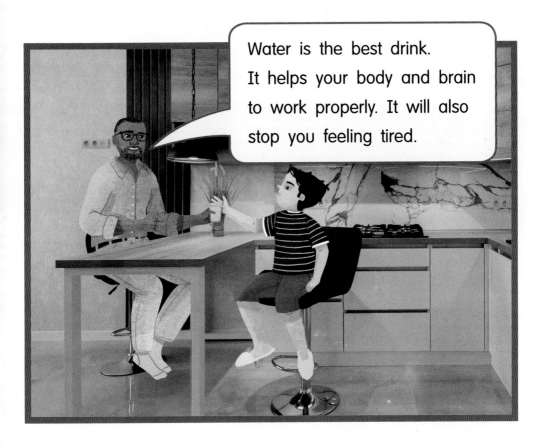

Water is the best drink. It helps your body and brain to work properly. It will also stop you feeling tired.

Fruit juice and smoothies are tasty, but Alex tells people to only have one small glass (150 ml) a day. He also tells people to only drink them at mealtimes to protect their teeth.

Helping hand

Doctors sometimes ask Alex to talk to unwell people about their diet.

Lucy has anaemia. Lucy's doctor sent her to see Alex so he can show her how to change her diet to make her feel better.

If a person has anaemia, they do not have enough iron in their blood. This can make them feel tired and breathless. A dietician may tell them to eat lots of iron-rich foods, such as green, leafy vegetables and lean meat.

Alex asks Lucy about her diet. He finds out what Lucy likes and does not like to eat. He also works out where Lucy can make improvements.

After speaking to Alex, Lucy changes her diet. She eats more foods containing iron.

What is an intolerance?

Ali visits Alex because whenever he drinks milk or eats some dairy foods, like yoghurt, he feels poorly.

Ali has an intolerance to **lactose**. Lactose is found in dairy foods like milk and cheese.

> An intolerance means a person cannot digest some types of food properly. Their bodies react badly to the food or its ingredients. This can make the person feel very unwell.

Alex takes Ali to the supermarket. He tells Ali about substitute foods he can try, such as soya milk or lactose-free cheese. By swapping milk and dairy foods for ones without lactose, Ali can enjoy the foods but not feel unwell!

Lactose is not the only food ingredient people can have an intolerance to. For example, some people have an intolerance to gluten (found in wheat) or caffeine (found in tea and coffee).

Helping fussy eaters

Sometimes Alex is asked to help families with a child who is a fussy eater.

A fussy eater is a child who refuses to eat certain foods, or may only eat one type of food, or will refuse to try anything new.

Lily and her family have come to Alex for help with Lily's diet. She only eats a few different foods and they are worried that she might get ill.

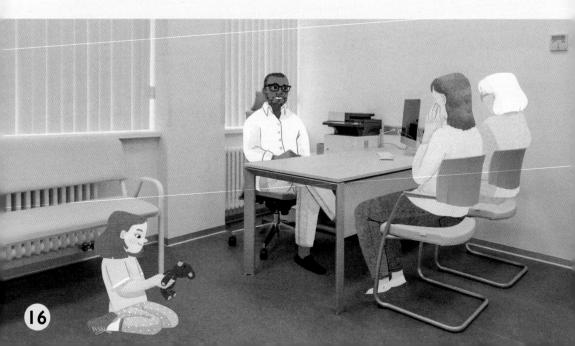

Alex assesses Lily's diet. He makes suggestions for how they can improve it to make sure she does not miss out on important nutrients. He shows Lily's family how to create a helpful mealtime routine.

It's important to eat meals at a similar time each day, and try not to rush them!

	Monday	Tuesday	Wednesday	Thursday	Friday
7.30am breakfast	Cereal with milk				
10am snack	Biscuit and dried fruit				
12pm lunch	Beans on toast				
3pm snack					
5pm dinner					

Sports diet

Because food is so important to how our bodies work, Alex also helps athletes to do better at their sports.

Alex advises the athletes to eat energy-giving foods such as bananas and raisins before they train or take part in competitions. Then they can go faster for longer.

Alex tells the rowers to eat lots of protein to become strong.

Alex tells the cyclist that a high-carbohydrate snack can quickly boost her energy levels.

Alex also talks to the children who play for a local football club. He tells them about good nutrients such as protein, calcium and carbohydrates.

Before the match, Alex tells them to eat a banana. Bananas contain carbohydrates which will give them energy.

At half-time he tells them to drink plenty of water. This will stop them getting **dehydrated**.

After the match, Alex tells them to drink a healthy milkshake. The milk contains protein and calcium to help their muscles recover.

Going into school

Sometimes Alex goes into schools to tell children about the foods that will help them to play and learn better.

What is best for breakfast?

He often begins by talking about breakfast. Alex asks the children to put up their hands if they ever skip breakfast. Some of the children raise their hands. Alex then asks the children if they ever feel tired at school, or if they find it hard to concentrate. Many of the same children raise their hands.

Alex explains that if we do not eat breakfast in the morning, we will not have the energy we need for our bodies and our brains to work.

Alex shows the children which foods are the best ones to have for breakfast.

Eggs, toast, orange juice, cereal with milk, fruit and yoghurt are all good breakfast foods. They give you nutrients so you can learn and play.

Stop feeling hungry

Alex also tells the children that it is important to eat a healthy lunch and dinner. Then they are less likely to feel hungry and snack on unhealthy foods.

Foods that are filled with fibre:

- wholemeal bread
- brown rice
- apples (with the peel on!)

- baked beans
- baked potatoes
- popcorn!

It's good to eat foods with fibre in them during every meal as they will fill us up and stop us feeling hungry.

Snack attack

Some snacks can make us feel hungry again very quickly.
Alex explains that fizzy drinks and sugary snacks do
not contain many nutrients or fibre. They can give us
a bit of instant energy, but that is soon used up. Alex
teaches the children about healthy, nutritious snacks to
eat instead.

Fruit and nuts are great snacks.
They give you energy but also fill
you up and stop you feeling hungry.

hazelnuts

almonds

walnuts

pistachios

Get involved!

Alex often asks children whether they help with the cooking at home. He tells children that helping with the cooking is a good way to learn more about healthy food. He even has some simple, healthy recipe ideas that children can try out, with just a little bit of help from a grown-up!

Try my tasty pitta bread pizzas with some salad! They make a nutritious lunch.

Pitta bread pizzas

Ingredients

6 wholemeal pitta breads

4 tablespoons passata

4 tablespoons tomato ketchup

150 g cherry tomatoes, halved

4 tablespoons sweetcorn

1 bell pepper, chopped up

75 g grated cheddar cheese

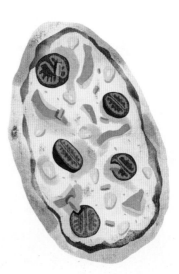

Method

Step 1: Toast the pitta breads.

Step 2: Mix the passata and ketchup in a bowl.

Step 3: Place the pitta breads on a baking tray and spoon on the sauce.

Step 4: Add the toppings, putting the cheese on last.

Step 5: Place under the grill until the cheese is bubbling.

The germ busters!

Alex teaches children about the importance of **hygiene**. He often takes children into the school kitchen. The first thing he tells them about is the importance of washing their hands. He explains that germs live on dirty hands and can get onto the food you pick up. Then the germs can get into your tummy when you eat and make you feel sick.

Bacteria from a child's hand.

Wash your hands ... and don't lick your fingers!

Alex explains that the school cooks use different coloured chopping boards for different foods. This is important so that foods, such as fruit and salads, do not become **contaminated** with raw meat or fish.

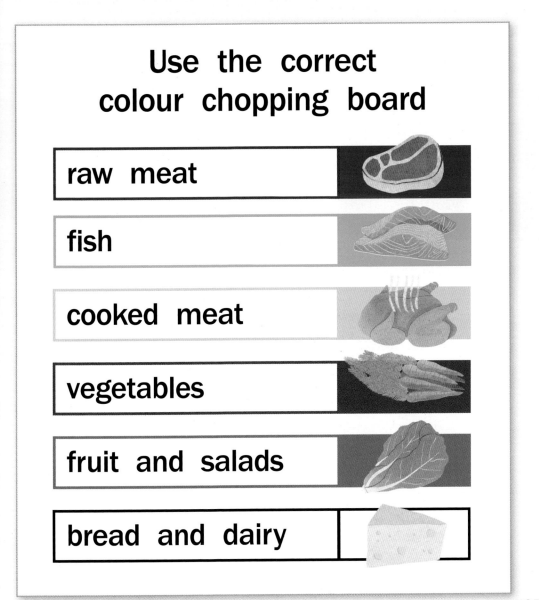

Use the correct colour chopping board

raw meat

fish

cooked meat

vegetables

fruit and salads

bread and dairy

Alex also talks to adults about food hygiene and how to keep food fresh and safe. He tells them where to keep food to stop it going bad or making you ill.

Rules for keeping food safe in the fridge:

- Keep the fridge at 5 degrees Celsius (°C) or below.

- Keep cooked food and dairy on the top two shelves.

- Keep raw meat and fish at the bottom so it does not drip onto other foods.

- Put leftovers in the fridge within two hours.

Alex also talks to adults about the importance of cooking foods properly. Some foods like chicken are dangerous to eat if they are not cooked properly first.

Did you know?

Cooking food properly can stop harmful bugs like salmonella getting into our bodies. Salmonella can make you very sick, causing stomach ache and vomiting.

You can use a thermometer to check the food has reached the right temperature. Chicken must be at least 75°C to be cooked.

Salmonella under a microscope.

Becoming a dietician

To become a dietician like Alex, you will need to:

- study science topics like nutrition and chemistry

- learn about how food affects the human body

- learn how to prepare and cook healthy, nutritious meals

- be interested in helping people to improve their diets and feel good

- be good at talking to people and working with them.

Glossary

contaminated: made poisonous

dehydrated: when someone has lost a lot of water from their body

diet: the food someone usually eats

digestion: how the stomach turns food into energy

hygiene: staying healthy and well by keeping things clean

lactose: a type of sugar

Index